night herding song

copper canyon press

night herding song

gerald hausman

port townsend 1979

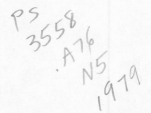

Thanks to the editors and publishers of the following magazines and anthologies for first publishing these poems:

Sam Hamill, Copper Canyon Press; Ward Abbot, Desert Review Press; Al Fogel, Sole Proprietor; David Kherdian, *Poetry Here and Now* (William Morrow); Alice May Brock, *My Life as a Restaurant* (Overlook Press); Gerard Malanga, *Cold Spring Journal*; Jean Malley and Hale Tokay, *Contemporaries: 28 New American Poets* (Viking), Harold Bond, *Ararat*.

Also thanks to the *Monterey News*, *The Second Berkshire Anthology*, Arts Action Press' Broadside Series.

Illustration by Sid Hausman

Special thanks to Centrum, where Copper Canyon is Press-in-residence, and to the National Endowment for the Arts for a grant which, in part, made this publication possible.

Copper Canyon Press
P.O. Box 271
Port Townsend, Washington 98368

Contents

I. Portraits

Night Herding Song / 7
Prayer for Red Meat / 8
The Travelers / 9
For Rainey, Alone on the Farm in Autumn / 11
Portrait of Myself in Wellman's Pond / 12
Wild Geese Again / 13
Leave Taking / 14
Night Hike in Napa / 15
Haircut / 16
Hills / 17
Summer at the Lake House / 18
Remembering Old Town / 19
Me / 20

II. Animals

Horse Moon / 23
Chicken Poem / 24
Vulture / 25
Inside the Bird Sanctuary / 26
Pigeons & Gulls / 27
Breath / 28
Mariah & the Owls / 29

III. Visions & Landscapes

Walking by the River / 33
Rug of Dawn / 34
Cleaning Out the Old Man's Well / 35
Umpachene Falls / 36
On the Banks of the Konkapot / 37
Bone Sermon / 38
Mariah's Night Mare / 39
Loom / 40
Burls / 41
A Question of Pears / 42
Watergods at Twelve Thousand Feet / 43
Balsam & Fern / 44
Aspen Meadows / 45
Rain in August / 46
Cherry Hill / 47
Tracks / 48
Clearing Trails / 49
Early Spring on Frog Creek Boulder / 50
Spring Barnyard Poem / 51
Hanna Hawkins / 52
Appaloosa Hail Storm / 53

I. PORTRAITS

Night Herding Song

Big horse in the meadow
stamps
shakes the burrs and fallen stars
from his mane.

His whinny comes across the field
coated with red leaves, moonlight,
early winter mist.

I hear him move in my sleep,
his hooves strum the soil
like a blind guitarist
on a river of silk.

Prayer for Red Meat

One night, when Old Moon was a bone awl
in a moccasin bag of stars
I dreamt of horns,
sang them in my sleep.

Then the white dream of an arrow
was my own hunger.

Sing thanks for bone, fat, meat
and thong.

Sing praise: my heart, my song.

The Travelers

When I arrived at his home
his mother witnessed
tired desert stars in my eyes,
          and she said:

"In the old country, when a traveler
came to us after a long journey,
we would bathe his feet
in soothing waters."

That was what she said,
and then I went to sleep
in crisp sheets with the door
partly open, so I could smell
the sprinklers and new mown grass.

A year passed, and my friend
visited my home in my absence,
and my uncle told him
the guest house was full,
and would he please sleep
in the barn where there
was an old cot
and the smell of rusty hinges.

I couldn't punish my uncle
when I returned, and feeling badly,
I mistakenly scolded my friend

whose feet were extremely tired
and in whose eyes I sensed
a memory of other betrayals:
scimitar moons, the courtyards of doom.

Yesterday, a postcard came to me
in the mail, and it said:

"It's so great to walk around in the sun
and disremember your troubles . . ."

And now I would bathe his feet
but it is years too late.

For Rainey, Alone on the Farm in Autumn

When you came last fall and said
the saws arrived
and workers with bright orange helmets
were cutting down the fruit trees,
I saw the reddish dust
like pollen in your hair.

You were lovely in your anger,
I wanted to hold you hard and say:
the orange hats are everywhere now.
But your tears and the saws
sang the same tune
and I said nothing
and that was the most
anyone would say.

Portrait of Myself in Wellman's Pond
from a photograph by Bob Totten

In one eye I see my father,
the man with the mustache
admiring the trees,
smiling in the weeds.
In the other eye I see my mother,
the woman who dove
off the cliffs of Maine
scattering the schools
of red-eyed muskelunge.

In my eyes I see them both
frozen like fern in stone.

Wild Geese Again

The last geese leaving
an unfinished song in the air
like musical chalk
on grey slate of sky.
I always call them quitters
as they hurry south, but now
with an armload of pine
and the back door open,
I haven't time to shout.

I put wood in the warm oven box,
breathe in the banana bread baking
in the stove, sit down
and begin to write.

Just then, the baby's whine.
I quit with the geese
on an undone line.

Leave Taking

I go around picking up
the fragments of her day
and find a yellow sock
the size of my thumb.

The coffee water whines
on the Coleman stove;
moths beat their fools' wings
against the screens.

When she waves herself nightly away
in my wife's arms,
it is only for a short while
but I feel the undertow.

As I sip my coffee
the final syllables of her world
spill out into a sugar bowl
of stars.

Night Hike in Napa

Stones sing under my feet
trees unbuckle their clothes
in the dark and dance.

My partner keeps ahead of me
by two steps—

Orion's belt
his sparkling headband.

Haircut

I feel you cutting my hair
brown strands
falling on my shoulders.
I dream of strange cafes
shadowy rooms
where old men mumble softly,
drunk.
When I come to,
the butterfly scissors
nip at my neck
hair drifts down shoulders
darkening
the light wood floor
with thick brown leaves.

Hills

I get merrier and merrier
with each foot step

rounds of poems
cranking away
inside my head
while my brother
ornery as a hot mule
practises banjo runs
on the neck of an old stick.

Summer at the Lake House

When dark comes
and motorboats die
I sit in the cabin
alone.

The mind whirls
I think of circle meadow
and the cave my mother
uncovered on the hill
when she was five.

Once more the snake hunters
return from black rock
with canoes full of timber rattlers,
grandfather snapper
surfaces in the dawn,
and the mohican council
sits by the graves of whippoorwills
smoking the last of their legends.

Remembering Old Town

Sitting on top of Griego's Cleaners
I showed you my first moon poem.

We watched the old tokay winos
fall asleep beside the Gallinas River.
We gathered gold cottonwood leaves
to line the blankets of our memory.

One night, when the Santa Fe freighter
switched tracks behind our house
we laid all our pennies on the line—
bright coppers, black silver rail.

Me

Crows and jays
jamming in the fruit trees
at sundown.

I just took a cold shower
stood naked
in the foggy mirror.

Me again
same face as this morning
twelve hours
and fifteen minutes
wiser.

II. ANIMALS

Horse Moon

Snowy horse head
shamed by the sun,
stamping
in our little glade
of yarrow.

I would ride her
but for the hail beat
of her hooves
in the apple boughs.

Chicken Poem

They wear spurs
they shine with sea brine

they come out of the sea
with pebbles of corn
caught in their beaks.

O chicken: lizard and bird
thrown into the same
sea wash of hay.

Vulture

Shadow's noise
as she floats over

great granddaughter
of the pterodactyl
your beast wings
bring momentary eclipse
to the sun.

I observe your sulking presence
in the open air
until you are nothing
but a sky notch,
a rifle sight.

Inside the Bird Sanctuary

Once I found three hemlocks
in a clearing
three stooped, gowned old women
holding hands
doing a circle dance.

I sat before them
knees tucked up to my chest:
the quiet held me
but there was something else—
the animals knew
deer and rabbit, dozens of tracks
signs or warnings
I left undisturbed
unread.

Pigeons & Gulls

Two ungraceful walkers, seagulls,
clack at crumbs
beside the fancy pigeons
of the park.

An old man sees the fools
and smiles, throws
a crust in the air.

The pigeons go up
like smoke in the flue
but it is the gulls'
feet-tucked, white-slanted flight
that takes final grace:
for a moment stopping the sun
in the fountains
and making all the old men
look up and sigh.

Breath

Behind the horse shed
three dark bays
and one shetland:
winter nostril breath,
eight white plumes.

Mariah *&* the Owls

Out at twilight, listening for owls,
my daughter and me.
She rides upon my shoulders
the way the moon rides
the bare haunch of a deer.

Listen, do you hear?

One sound plaited upon another.
Darkness, the Shadow Weaver.

Moon whinnies on the hillside
but no owls.
The bellow of a distant cow,
cars, creaking branches, far off dogs
barking, but no owls.

Then it comes: a shrilly whimper
one, and then another
and that is all.
A young screech owl has flown
home to its mate
with a mouse in its claws.

I stand up. Cold sneakers,
rush of blood returning to my body.
The weight on my shoulders
is sound asleep and snoring.

Mariah, did you hear? Silence.
The walk home, and then I put
her to bed, clothes and all.
She blinks in the glare of a table light.

"Daddy," she says, at once, wide awake
"I heard that owl," and falls back asleep.

III. VISIONS AND LANDSCAPES

Walking by the River

Our wives stayed by the fire
while we walked down by the river
and counted wrens' nests
in the rose hip briars.

"There's a bird," you said
"that lives around here,
whose nest always
has a snakeskin woven
into it."

Downstream was the falls;
under rock ledges damp autumn mice
huddled in milkweed pods
for the night.

I thought I saw new wrinkles
around your eyes,
but then I laughed
and felt my own
multiply like river whorls.

Come, unknown and nameless bird—
sleep in our wrinkled eyes
and be the weaver of our lost skins.

Rug of Dawn

Dawn on a mesa top:
I opened one eye
and saw the whole sky
    a Navajo loom
with the lavender flower
of distance
thinning the edges—
    treadle, shuttle, weave.

Old Coyote, dawn stealer
in the first days of life,
sorrowing at the center
of all things dark
with his outrageous heart;
    laughing, laughing
      at the sun—
a memory too hot
to hold
on even
his tricky tongue.

Cleaning Out the Old Man's Well

There is always the fear
of who I am down there

me stuck in that hole—
the sink a man put
in a green field
to feed his blue eyes

I stare crazily up
at my helpers
who, on the very rim of sky
toss a rope
into the hole's blue eye.

Umpachene Falls

Once when Umpachene was a secret
shared with the pines
I leaped to the carp deep river
swam like an otter
to a singing cave
behind the falls.

Now the noon sun
shines
on coke bottle fangs
sunk in sand.

On the Banks of the Konkapot

She uncurled herself
from her clothes
as easily as emerald snakes
slip from the claws
of tufted owls.

Bone Sermon

Take a bone
hold it in your hand:
a bone held by a bone.

Dig a well
bring up a shell:
a sea bone.

Man is at home
with so many bones.

Mariah's Night Mare

Comet tails
sizzle and growl
in borders
corners
crevices:
those midnight places
where dark
broods
moodily at light.

Loom

Hiding myself
in the shadows of peepers and owls,
I watch the whitened stems of days
lead underground,
go swiftly down without a breath.
Here are the smallest of lives—
voices woven, season after season,
in the quiet loom of the leaf.

Burls

Maple burls like rounded knots of rope.
Drinking cups, the early settlers
carried them on their belts.
A curious find:
dark eyes
of a tree
grown blind.

A Question of Pears

Why did I want to write
about gold pears this morning?

Because one neighbor's mowing
his lawn
and the other
is dismantling his porch?

And I have neither
mower nor porch?

(Nor even golden pears:
they're mud brown in the sun.)

Watergods at Twelve Thousand Feet

Water craters
spread upon the lake
and I saw fat brown-legged fish
with heads of curious puppies.

Faint purple-fanning gills,
slow underwater flowers
that broke the surface
one second before the rain
fell into icy daggers
that cut my face.

Balsam & Fern

Dusk, and the cat comes in,
down the steep moss and weed-
hung stone wall behind our
house. I breathe her fur
as she sleeps on the bed
and it is warm with balsam
and fern, and wet in places
with damp strange life
close to the ground.

Aspen Meadows

We drink where the deer drink,
half-moon prints
pressed into soft black mud.
I lean my face low
to the rock well, last of summer
water driven deep in the ground.
A moment later I see my reflection
then the dark chill
enters my throat:
when my eyes close
I see aspen leaves
shake pale green above my head.

Rain in August

A fireplace log
bares red teeth.
White petals
shrink in the heat
of my lamp.
All day hiss
of rain in pines.

A frog in the middle
of the floor
croaks goodbye
to motorboat madness
and the summer people's sun.

Cherry Hill

At tamarack swamp,
spiny needles
small conical house
with snow roof
half-fallen in.

I can make out stones,
silence of no season
at the bottom of the black
well inside.

Deep down
a lone eel
carves our silence
into a fin's holy gesture.

Tracks

I walk on blue river ice
mouse or weasel tracks
scattered like seeds in the snow.

Stop to look at the curved
diamond pattern of cat prints:
strange, isolate, they smell
at once animal.

Now mine are hours old
in night time frost,
webbed snowshoe marks
giving off
a dark human odor
hotter
than an uptailed skunk.

Clearing Trails

Rain stopped us, we three
huddled
under our horses
rain water down tails
thin streams on flanks

long brown horse head
between pines
huge patient body
steaming over me
as we swap stories,
wait out the rain.

Early Spring on Frog Creek Boulder

White wine and bonfire sparks.
We dance and sing
on old bullfrog's head—
frozen belly full of honeyed gnats.

A year and I am older, softer
no longer willing to argue.

Only old bullfrog stays the same
with his indifferent smile
of secret promise.

All of us laughing and singing
freezing and melting:
happy little gnats
on Frog Creek Boulder.

Spring Barnyard Poem

Two horses nibble snow
blackbirds, golden manure kings

cherry tree splits
thru barn roof

horse over my shoulder
bares spring green teeth
splintering blackbirds

Hanna Hawkins

Cowbones shut in a root cellar
gone under.
The old house, an ash heap
these fifty years.

Where do we look
for the little girl's bones
buried so long ago
in the orchard sun?

Look to the fern
as it nods itself
to sleep, look
to the weeds that come
up like yesterday's children.

Appaloosa Hail Storm

Hauled hay bales all afternoon
saddle blankets, wet with sweat
dry on fence in the sun.

Stalls full, one wheelbarrow load
of hot sweet manure
tips on thin plank out back.

Suddenly the sky is all summer storm.
I sit on my overturned wheelbarrow
and watch an appaloosa explode into hail.

Gerald Hausman is the author of several books of poetry including *Circle Meadow*, *New Marlboro Stage*, and *Sitting on the Blue-Eyed Bear*. He lives in an owner-built adobe house near Tusuque, New Mexico.

This book was designed by Sam Hamill and Tree Swenson at Copper Canyon Press. The type is Trump Mediaeval and was designed by Georg Trump. Typesetting by Irish Setter, Portland, Oregon. 1000 copies are sewn into paper wrappers, and 50 copies case-bound in cloth over boards and signed by the poet.